Department of Health

Eighth Report of the Committee for Monitoring Agreements on

Tobacco Advertising and Sponsorship

Chairman:
Sir Clive Whitmore, GCB CVO

London: HMSO

Committee for Monitoring Agreements on Tobacco Advertising and Sponsorship

PO Box 3982, London SE1 8YJ

Chairman: Sir Clive Whitmore GCB CVO

Joint Secretaries: Mrs Gill Silverman, Tel: 0171 630 9749
Ms Rosamond Roughton, Tel: 0171 972 4220

Your Reference:

Our Reference:
Date:

23rd June, 1995

The Rt Hon Virginia Bottomley JP MP
Secretary of State for Health
Department of Health
Richmond House
79 Whitehall
London
SW1A 2NS

Dear Secretary of State,

I submit the Eighth Report of the Committee for Monitoring Agreements on Tobacco Advertising and Sponsorship (COMATAS).

The period covered by our report was marked by the coming into effect of two new voluntary agreements between the Government and the tobacco industry. Both the agreement of November 1992 on advertising and promotion and the agreement of January 1987 on the sponsorship of sport by tobacco companies were replaced with new agreements in December 1994 and January 1995 respectively. Their main provisions are summarised at Annexes A and B of our report, and we are now monitoring their operation.

The past year has been a busy one for the Committee. As Part 2 of the report explains, we received 39 letters of complaint describing 50 items which the writers thought might be breaches of the agreement on advertising and promotion. These figures represent a sharp increase over the 8 letters and 36 items mentioned in the Committee's Seventh Report. But I am pleased to say that only 14 were considered by the Committee to be breaches of the agreement (in comparison with 17 the year before).

During the renegotiation of the voluntary agreement there was a certain amount of media coverage, and this may well have prompted an increase in the number of complaints to us. We have also made an effort this year to publicise the work of the Committee more widely. In March I wrote to a wide variety of organisations, including health authorities and chief education officers, to bring the new agreements to their attention. I welcome the heightened awareness of the Committee's work.

1994/95 has seen a considerable change in the make-up of the complaints in terms of the advertising medium concerned. As table 2.1 of our report shows, about half of the complaints involved posters - usually posters thought to be within sight of schools or other places of education. None of the complaints concerned advertisements in shops. The previous year, on the other hand, over three-quarters of the complaints were about advertisements in shops and only one-sixth about posters. I find it difficult to be sure about the reasons for this change, but the explanation may lie in a combination of two factors. The first is that under successive agreements the industry has been steadily reducing the amount of permanent shop front advertising. And the second is that the prohibition on poster advertising within 200 metres of schools is one of the main new provisions of the latest agreement, and this may have focused attention on this area and so stimulated complaints.

A common feature of past reports has been the acceptance by the Committee that a number of the complaints found to be breaches were "inadvertent" breaches, for example, where a poster management company acting on behalf of a tobacco company put up a poster within sight of a school. The tobacco companies have now agreed that they will take responsibility for the actions of their contractors and that breaches committed by such contractors will no longer be treated as inadvertent. I think that this is a useful change of classification and I see the tobacco companies' decision as a measure of the seriousness with which they regard the voluntary agreement.

The Committee has expressed concern in the past about the time taken to deal with complaints and has encouraged efforts to reduce it. During the period covered by the Seventh Report the turn-round time was twelve weeks: last year it was halved to six weeks. Both the tobacco companies and the Committee's Secretariat deserve credit for this improvement.

The Committee's activities are now of course focussed on monitoring the operation of the new voluntary agreements. Over the coming year we shall arrange three studies designed to gauge how the industry is complying with certain of the provisions of the agreement on advertising and promotion. The first check will be on the tobacco companies' undertaking to have withdrawn by 1st January, 1995 all outdoor advertising for their products (excluding signs at retail premises) within a radius of 200 metres from the front entrance of schools and other places of education for young people under 18. Second, we shall assess whether the provisions of the cigarette sampling code are being upheld and in particular whether the principle that samples should not be offered to non-smokers and under-18 year olds is being observed. Finally, we have agreed that an audit should be carried out later in the year to measure progress towards the industry's target of removing all permanent shop front advertising by the end of 1996.

I succeeded Sir John Blelloch as Chairman of the Committee at the beginning of the year and I should like to take the opportunity to pay a very warm tribute to him for all that he did to enable the Committee to do its job effectively. I must also echo what he said in submitting the Seventh Report about the industry's continuing commitment to the letter and spirit of the voluntary agreements. Coming new to the work of the Committee I have been much encouraged by the positive and constructive way in which my colleagues from both Government and the industry approach the task of monitoring the agreements.

Yours sincerely,

Clive Whitmore.

Sir Clive Whitmore

Contents

Page Nos

1. Introduction   1

2. Analysis of Responses to Complaints on Tobacco Advertising   5

3. Restrictions on Advertising in Young Women's Magazines   8

4. Sports Sponsorship   10

5. Financial Aspects of the Agreements   11

6. Independent Investigations Commissioned by the Committee   13

Annex A: Main provisions of the Agreement on Tobacco Products' Advertising and Promotion, published in December 1994

Annex B: Main provisions of the Agreement on Sponsorship of Sport by Tobacco Companies (Agreed in January 1995)

EIGHTH REPORT OF THE COMMITTEE FOR
MONITORING AGREEMENTS ON TOBACCO
ADVERTISING AND SPONSORSHIP

1. Introduction

The Committee for Monitoring Agreements on Tobacco Advertising and
Sponsorship (COMATAS) was set up under the terms of the Voluntary Agreement
on Tobacco Products' Advertising and Promotion and Health Warnings, concluded
on 1 April 1986 between HM Government and the United Kingdom tobacco industry
as represented by the Tobacco Advisory Council, now the Tobacco Manufacturers
Association (TMA), and the Imported Tobacco Products Advisory Council (ITPAC).

2.   A new agreement on advertising and promotion was published on 9 September
1991 and revised on 1 January 1992 to reflect the requirements of the EC Directive
on tobacco products labelling.   The agreement was replaced in November 1992 by
a new agreement in identical terms, save for an additional clause designed to ensure
compliance with the Restrictive Trade Practices Act 1976.   In May 1994 the
Government and the Industry agreed a new package of measures on advertising and
promotion, and these formed the basis of a new voluntary agreement which was
published in December 1994 and which came into effect on 1st January 1995.

Terms of Reference   3.   The Committee's task is to monitor the operation of the Voluntary Agreement
on Tobacco Products' Advertising and Promotion, and the Voluntary Agreement on
Sponsorship of Sport by Tobacco Companies in the UK concluded in January 1995
(see chapter 4).   Summaries of the main provisions of these Agreements are to be
found in Annexes A and B.

4.   The Committee's terms of reference are set out in Appendix 8 to the Voluntary
Agreement on Advertising and Promotion and are as follows:

"a.   To keep under review all matters relating to the operation of the voluntary
agreement other than those relating directly to the operation of the Cigarette
Code which are supervised by the Advertising Standards Authority, or matters
which are the responsibility of the BBC or ITC.

b. To ensure that the terms of the voluntary agreement are properly observed and are interpreted with consistency.

c. To receive full details of all complaints sent by the public or public bodies to the Government Department concerned, and of the responses by those companies to whom the complaints were referred. In the case of disputed matters or those which raise general issues relevant to the observance of the agreement, to take a view and, where appropriate, communicate that view to the parties concerned.

d. To report annually to Ministers, and to member companies through the TMA and ITPAC respectively, on the general implementation of the agreement".

Method of Working

5. The Committee is required to meet as often as business demands and at least quarterly. Its first meeting was in December 1986 and it has so far met a total of thirty-nine times, four since the publication of the Seventh Annual Report in August 1994. In keeping with the rules set out in the Agreement on Advertising and Promotion its proceedings are confidential except that its annual report may be published at the discretion of Ministers following consultation with the tobacco industry. After consultation with the tobacco industry, and with the complete agreement of the Committee, the seven previous annual reports have been published. The Committee is serviced by a joint secretariat provided by the Government and the Tobacco Manufacturers Association.

6. The Committee arranges for the investigation of complaints submitted by the public. In most cases the relevant company is asked to carry out an investigation and report back to the Committee, although in some cases the Secretariat investigates. The Committee then takes a view. The Committee decided at an early stage that to rely solely on the random incidence of complaints as a measure of compliance by the industry would not be sufficient to assure itself that the agreement was being upheld. Accordingly, in order to provide a more systematic basis for evaluation and in line with its remit, the Committee commissions independent consultants to investigate how certain aspects of the agreements are being adhered to. The Committee has so far commissioned eleven studies:

i. health warnings on shop-front advertising (two studies);

ii.   the location of cigarette and hand-rolling tobacco brand advertising on posters in relation to schools;

iii. general aspects of two televised sporting events sponsored by tobacco companies;

iv.   adherence to the Cigarette Promotion Code (which forms part of the voluntary agreement) with specific reference to direct mail;

v.   audit of permanent shopfront advertising to establish the base figure for 1 July 1991 from which the 50 per cent reduction over 5 years would take place, as detailed in the 1991 Agreement;

vi.   an audit each year subsequently of progress towards the 50 per cent reduction in permanent shopfront advertising (three studies);

vii. two annual surveys to assess whether the industry had met its undertaking not to replace permanent shopfront advertising material for cigarettes and hand-rolling tobacco with permanent advertising material for other tobacco products or with similar non-permanent signs for any tobacco products.

The results of the first four studies were presented in the first two Annual Reports. The study of direct mail procedures was reported in the Fourth and Fifth Annual Reports. Details of the baseline audit of permanent shopfront advertising and the first audit of progress towards the 50 per cent reduction were included in the Sixth Report. The Seventh Annual Report recorded the second audit of progress on reducing permanent shopfront advertising, and the first survey to verify that permanent advertising had not been replaced with temporary signs. Chapter 6 of this Report summarises the results of the two most recent studies.

Membership   7.   The Committee is composed of equal numbers of representatives of the Government departments concerned and the tobacco industry, under an independent Chairman appointed with the agreement of Ministers and the Chairman of the Tobacco Manufacturers Association. The current Chairman, Sir Clive Whitmore GCB CVO, was appointed from 1 January 1995. As at 1 June 1995 the Committee members were:

Sir Clive Whitmore GCB CVO Chairman

Mr G Podger (DH)	Mr D Swan (TMA)
Ms L Lockyer (DH)	Mr D R Hare (TMA)
Mr E Miller (Scottish Office)	Mr I E Birks (Gallaher Ltd)
Mr A G Thornton (Welsh Office)	Ms J Smithson (Rothmans International)
Mr D Baker (DHSS NI)	Mr P L C Middleton (Imperial Tobacco Ltd)
Miss A Stewart (DNH)	Mr K Varma (R J Reynolds)
	Mr R Loader (ITPAC)

Joint Secretaries

Ms R Roughton (DH)	Mrs G Silverman (TMA)

8.   The Committee thanks Sir John Blelloch, who left at the end of 1994, for his work as Chairman.   It would also like to thank Mr Daniel Oxberry of Rothmans (UK) Ltd who left the Committee after serving on it from its inception for his contribution to its work.   The Committee thanks Mr Strachan Heppell of the Department of Health, Mr Kevin Jewsbury of R J Reynolds, and the previous Secretary Mr Ben Dyson (DH).

Finances

9.   The Committee is funded jointly by the Government and the Industry.   In the period 1 February 1994 to 31 January 1995 committed expenditure (including VAT) was as follows:

Permanent Shopfront Audit & signage survey	£54,425.59
Chairman's fees	£2,000.00
Postbox	£100.00

Members' and Secretaries' expenses were met by their Department or Company. The Chairman's fees were increased to £3,000 per year from 1 April 1995.

4

2 Analysis of Responses to Complaints on Tobacco Advertising

Sources of Complaints

1. During its eighth year the Committee received thirty nine letters of complaint about the voluntary agreement on tobacco advertising and thirty four queries. Nineteen letters of complaint were from private individuals, eleven were from health bodies, four were from schools, two were from local authorities, two from MPs on behalf of private individuals and one was from a voluntary organisation. These figures refer to the period 1 June 1994 to 31 May 1995 inclusive.

Nature of Complaints

2. The letters of complaint gave details of 50 items which were thought to be possible breaches of the voluntary agreement on advertising and promotion. Nearly half of these concerned posters carrying tobacco advertising within close proximity to schools or other places of education. Other concerns raised were the choice of health warnings in magazine advertisements and the nature of promotional offers. Six items concerned the promotion and advertising of cigarettes at a motor show.

Table 2.1 *Complaints: advertising medium*

Posters	26
Press	9
Promotions	8
Vehicles	3
Point-of-sale	3
Beer mats	1
TOTAL	50

Committee Conclusions

3.   The Committee concluded that fourteen items had been in breach of the agreement, although eight were defined as inadvertent breaches where the tobacco company was not held to be directly responsible for the breach.   Seven of these concerned the location of posters carrying tobacco advertising within the sight of schools or other places of education.   This was deemed to be the responsibility of the poster management companies.   The eighth inadvertent breach occurred when the health warning on an advertisement at the point of sale was not visible, owing to the actions of the retailer.

4.   During the course of the year the Committee clarified the definition of inadvertent breaches.   It has now been agreed by the tobacco companies that they will take responsibility for all actions taken by a sub-contractor such as a poster company and that in future such breaches would not be defined as inadvertent.

5. Since the change in definition, of the six further breaches five occurred when posters carrying tobacco advertising were placed within the close proximity of schools or other places of education.   These previously would have been defined as inadvertent.   In all such cases, the advertisements were taken down immediately. The remaining item concerned the lack of a health warning on advertising at the point of sale at a motor show.

6.   In twenty five cases, there had been no breach.   In a further two cases, the Committee was unable to reach a conclusion on the basis of the evidence presented to it.   Eight items were outside the scope of the voluntary agreement: three of these related to advertisements in international magazines which are not covered by the agreement.   One concerned the carrying of advertising on models of motor vehicles on display at a motor show.   These models had been provided by the motor car companies (the tobacco companies had not been involved) and therefore fell outside the scope of the agreement.   One item concerned the sponsorship of a musical event: this is not covered in the agreement.   The remaining three items concerned advertising for products other than tobacco products.   One complaint is still under investigation.

Table 2.2 *Committee Conclusions*

Items in breach	14 (8 inadvertent)
Items not in breach	25
Insufficient evidence to reach a conclusion	2
Items outside the scope of the agreement	8
Under investigation	1
TOTAL	50

Time taken to respond to complaints

5.　The Secretariat instigate immediate investigations of all complaints received by the Committee, except where they clearly fall outside the scope of the agreement. However, it is not always possible to send a final reply to the complainant until after the Committee has reached a view on the complaint at one of its quarterly meetings. Since the Seventh Annual Report was published, the average time taken to deal with complaints (including those about sports sponsorship) has been six weeks.

3 Restrictions on Advertising in Young Women's Magazines

1. The voluntary agreement on advertising and promotion provides that advertisements for cigarettes or hand-rolling tobacco will not be placed in magazines for which the female readership aged 15-24 is 25 per cent or more of the total adult readership.

2. The following table lists those magazines which, on the basis of average readership figures for the four quarters ending March 1995, should not carry cigarette or hand-rolling tobacco advertising. Any newly published magazine or periodical may not carry such advertising until the readership figures for the first six months have been established, unless it can be established by other figures or bases accepted by the monitoring committee that the criteria do not apply.

Table 3.1   *Young Women's Magazines: 1995 Proscribed Publications List*

Publications whose female readership aged 15-24 exceeds
25% of total adult readers (aged 15 and above)

Title	% Female readership aged 15-24
Looks	81
Catch	77
Mizz	72
Nineteen	71
More!	67
Just Seventeen	56
Big!	52
Company	49
Shout	47
Clothes Show Magazine	43
Smash Hits	40
Elle	37
New Woman	36
Hair Flair	35
Hair	31
Wedding & Home	30
Flicks	30
Marie Claire	30
OK! Magazine	29
Cosmopolitan	28
Vogue	27
Eva	27
The Face	26

DDS/NRS Readership Survey, April 1994 - March 1995

9

4 Sports Sponsorship

1.   A new voluntary agreement on sports sponsorship was published in January 1995, to replace the previous agreement (dated January 1987). Its main provisions are set out in Annex B.

2.   The Seventh Report recorded one outstanding complaint concerning the use of a cigarette brand logo on the equipment and cars of participants in a televised motor racing event.   The Committee concluded that there had been no breach of the agreement, because the company involved was foreign and not party to the agreement.   However it was noted that, since the complaint had been made, the company had now signed up to the Sonning Agreement by which European tobacco manufacturing associations and their members have agreed to recognise voluntary agreements in other Member States.

3.   In the last year, the Committee received one letter of complaint[1] and two queries in respect of sports sponsorship. The complaint concerned signs at a motor show promoting a motor racing team sponsored by a tobacco manufacturer. The Committee did not find them to be in breach of the agreement.

4.   As in previous years, each tobacco company fulfilled the undertaking in the voluntary agreement to notify the Department of National Heritage of its sponsorship plans for the year ahead and any subsequent changes to those plans.

---

[1]. This letter also contained some complaints about advertising and so has been included in the total number of letters about the voluntary agreement on tobacco advertising.

5 Financial Aspects of the Agreements

Advertising expenditure

1. The agreements require the Tobacco Manufacturers Association and the Imported Tobacco Products Advisory Council to supply the Government in confidence with annual figures on industry expenditure on press and poster advertising and on sports sponsorship.

2. As in previous years, the figures supplied by the Tobacco Manufacturers Association for the year ending 31 March 1994 were certified by an auditor. Each company sent its figures, accompanied by a certificate from its auditors, to the Tobacco Manufacturers Association. These figures were aggregated, and the Tobacco Manufacturers Association's auditors then certified that the aggregate figure was an accurate sum of the figures from the individual companies. The aggregated figures were then sent to the Department of Health or (in the case of sports sponsorship) the Department of National Heritage, accompanied by the auditor's certificate.

Limit on spending on cigarette brand poster advertising

3. The September 1991 voluntary agreement on tobacco products' advertising and promotion governs the industry expenditure on press and poster advertising in 1993/94. The terms state that:

"The companies represented by the Tobacco Manufacturers Association will continue to limit their expenditure on cigarette brand poster advertising in each successive twelve month period from 1 April 1991 to 50% in aggregate of the level in the year ending 31 March 1980, subject to allowances for inflation as agreed with the DH.

"The companies represented by the Imported Tobacco Products Advisory Council will ensure that the expenditure on poster advertising of cigarette brands that they import does not exceed 3.5% in aggregate of the limit accepted by the Tobacco Manufacturers Association for the twelve month period ending 31 March in each year of the agreement."

4.   The figures from the Tobacco Manufacturers Association (certified by the auditors) for cigarette brand poster advertising in 1993/94 show that expenditure was within the total permitted spend after making allowances for inflation.   The Department of Health has informed the Committee that, on the basis of the figures supplied by the Imported Tobacco Products Advisory Council, the amount spent by their members on cigarette brand poster advertising was within the agreed expenditure limit.

Limit on spending on sports sponsorship

5.   The voluntary agreement on sports sponsorship published in January 1987 governs the limits for the amount to be spent on sports sponsorship by individual companies during the financial year 1993/4.   The aggregated data provided by the Tobacco Manufacturers Association, and certified by audit, show that expenditure on sports sponsorship for the year 1993/94 was within the allowed spend using 1985 as a base year and that the proportion of total expenditure spent on media advertising and other promotional material directly related to the events, otherwise than at events, was less than 20 per cent.

6 Independent Investigations Commissioned by the Committee

Audit of Permanent Shopfront Material

1.   Under the earlier agreement on advertising and promotion (published September 1991) the industry undertook to reduce the total number of permanent advertising signs for cigarette and hand-rolling tobacco brands at retail premises by 50 per cent over five years. The agreement requires the industry to take all reasonable steps to ensure that the reduction is applied evenly over time, by type of sign and by geographic location. Priority should be given to reducing the number of permanent signs on shops clearly visible from schools.

2.   Coopers and Lybrand were appointed to carry out an annual independent audit to monitor progress in this undertaking. The audit in 1993 (reported in the Seventh Annual Report) indicated that permanent shopfront advertising for cigarettes and hand-rolling tobacco had declined by at least 20 per cent for every category of sign and by geographic location. The percentage of signs visible from schools had decreased by 83 per cent from the audit base.

3.   In 1994 Coopers and Lybrand undertook a further audit to validate progress towards the targets. The auditors again reviewed the companies' systems for collecting, holding, and amending their records of permanent signs. From these records the companies provided the auditors with information about the reduction made in the year from July 1993. The auditors tested the accuracy of this information by a sample of visits to over 350 retail outlets.

4.   The 1994 audit indicated that external permanent advertising signs for cigarettes and hand-rolling tobacco at retail premises had declined by over 30 per cent from the 1991 audit base for every category of sign and by geographic location. The number of signs clearly visible from schools had fallen by 94 per cent from the audit base. The auditors declared these figures as representing fairly, in all material respects, the situation of external permanent cigarette and hand-rolling tobacco advertising signs at retail premises in July 1994 and the decrease from the 1991 audit base.

**Survey of replacement
of permanent signage**

5.   The industry made a further commitment in 1992 not to replace:

i.   external permanent advertising signs with similar non-permanent signs for any tobacco products;

ii. such permanent cigarette shopfront advertising material with permanent advertising for other tobacco products.

6.   Coopers and Lybrand carried out a survey in 1993 to ensure that the industry had met this undertaking. A similar survey was carried out in 1994. The auditors selected a sample of 100 sites from which permanent advertising had been removed. They visited these sites to check whether permanent material had been replaced with similar non-permanent material or with permanent advertisements for other tobacco products. For the purposes of the survey, similarity between permanent and non-permanent material was defined in terms of its impact, its extent or coverage, and the materials used.

7.   There was no evidence from the auditors' survey that external permanent advertising signs for cigarettes or hand-rolling tobacco had been replaced with similar non-permanent signs or with advertising for other tobacco products.

VOLUNTARY AGREEMENT ON TOBACCO ADVERTISING AND PROMOTION

Introduction

The voluntary agreement sets out rules for the advertising and promotion of tobacco products. It is an agreement between UK Health Ministers and the manufacturers and importers of tobacco products in the UK. The current agreement will stand until at least 1 June 1999, with provision for amendment in the light of any UK legislation necessary to enact EC legislation.

The agreement covers two main areas:

    i.   the content of cigarette advertisements;

    ii.   the placement of tobacco advertisements, limits on expenditure, promotional activities, the use of health warnings, and related matters.

Content of cigarette advertisements

The content of advertisements for cigarettes, cigarette papers and hand-rolling tobacco, including special offers and related sales promotions, is controlled by the Cigarette Code which comes under the supervision of the Advertising Standards Authority. The Code includes the following requirements:

- no advertisement should incite people to start smoking or, if they are already smokers, to increase their consumption;

- advertisements should never suggest that smoking is safe, healthy, natural, necessary for relaxation or concentration, or popular;

- smoking should not be associated with social, sexual, romantic or business success;

- advertisements should not employ any approach which is more likely to attract the attention or sympathy of those under 18;

- humour is acceptable provided it is used with care and is not likely to have a particular appeal to the young;

- advertisements should not associate smoking with sport or with active or outdoor games. Advertisements for sporting events sponsored by UK tobacco companies are governed separately by the voluntary agreement on sports sponsorship.

Any public complaints about the content of cigarette advertisements should be sent to:

The Advertising Standards Authority
Brook House
2-16 Torrington Place
LONDON WC1E 7HN

Placement of advertisements

The main rules that apply to the placement of advertisements are:

- there will be no cigarette or hand-rolling tobacco brand advertising on posters which are smaller than 48 sheet (120" by 240") from 1 January 1995;

- there will be no cigarette or hand-rolling tobacco advertising on the exterior of vehicles. This will take effect for public vehicles (eg buses and taxis) from 1 January 1995;

- all poster advertising for all tobacco products within 200 metres of the front entrance of schools and other places of education for young people under 18 years of age will be withdrawn by 1 January 1995. In addition, no poster advertising for cigarettes or hand-rolling tobacco should be clearly visible from and clearly identifiable from within such establishments;

- all permanent shopfront advertising material for all tobacco products will be removed by 31 December 1996. The industry will not replace this permanent material with non-permanent material that is similar in terms of its impact, its extent or coverage, or the materials used;

- no advertisements should appear in any publication aimed wholly or mainly at a readership under 18 years of age, nor should they appear in magazines where 25% or more of the adult readership (aged 15 or over) are young women between the ages of 15-24;

- advertising cigarette brands or hand-rolling tobacco at cinemas or on rental or retail video cassettes is not allowed;

- tobacco advertising is not allowed on computer games or on any other computer equipment or software.

Expenditure on poster advertising

Annual expenditure on cigarette brand poster advertising will be limited to 30% of the 1980 expenditure level, allowing for inflation, from April 1995.

Promotional activities

Promotional offers should be confined to adult smokers aged 18 or over. Companies will adhere to the "Cigarette Promotion Code" and the "Cigarette Sampling Code" which include the following:

- companies should avoid using promotional material which will appeal more particularly to young people than to the public at large;

- all promotional letters and leaflets containing offers should bear a prominent statement that the offer is restricted to smokers aged 18 and over, and all application forms for promotional offers should require the applicant to sign a statement that he or she is a smoker aged 18 or over;

- special care should be taken to avoid offering free samples of cigarettes or hand-rolling tobacco to non-smokers or anyone aged under 18. Where a company wishes to offer samples at an organised event, it should establish in advance that at least 70% of those expected to attend will be adults aged 18 or over.

Health warnings

All new press and poster advertisements and shop advertising material for all tobacco products will carry a health warning. The main rules on the use of health warnings are:

- press and poster advertisements for all tobacco products will carry the health warnings which are required by law to appear by rotation on packets. The warnings shall also be used in rotation in advertisements;

- the area of press and poster advertisements used for the health warning will be 20% for cigarette and hand-rolling tobacco brands and 10% for cigar and pipe tobacco brands;

- the presentation of warnings on cigarette and hand-rolling tobacco advertisements will be evenly rotated between white lettering on a black background and black lettering on a white background;

- new permanent promotional material (ashtrays, jugs, ice buckets and beer mats) for cigarettes and hand-rolling tobacco will also carry a general health warning;

- advertising material in duty-free areas, airline and shipping line magazines and newspapers or magazines with more than 80% of the circulation overseas are excluded from the agreement.

Monitoring

The Committee for Monitoring Agreements on Tobacco Advertising and Sponsorship (COMATAS) will commission independent studies to monitor compliance with the voluntary agreement.

In addition, COMATAS will investigate and respond to complaints about possible breaches of the voluntary agreement, other than complaints about the content of advertisements which should be addressed to the ASA. The COMATAS address is:

The Secretariat
COMATAS
PO Box 3982
LONDON SE1 8YJ

Copies of the agreement can be obtained from the COMATAS secretariat.

VOLUNTARY AGREEMENT ON THE SPONSORSHIP OF SPORT BY TOBACCO COMPANIES IN THE UK

Introduction

The voluntary agreement sets out the rules for the sponsorship of sport by tobacco companies. It is an agreement between the Minister for Sport, the Tobacco Manufacturers Association (TMA) and the Imported Tobacco Products Advisory Council (ITPAC). The current agreement was published on 31 January 1995.

The principal features of the agreement are:

- Tobacco companies shall not sponsor sporting activities where the majority of the participants or of the target audience is under 18.

Expenditure

- The agreement caps the total amount of expenditure by tobacco companies on sports sponsorship to 1985 levels (in real terms).

- The maximum amount tobacco companies can spend on promoting a sponsored event is 15 per cent of their total sponsorship expenditure. In other words at least 85 per cent of tobacco spending on sponsorship must go directly to the events themselves.

Health warnings

- All press and poster advertising for sponsored events has to carry a health warning covering 20 per cent of the total area.

- Static promotional signs at both televised and non-televised sponsored events have to carry health warnings covering 20 per cent of the total area.

Advertising and promotion of sponsored events

- Cinema advertising of sponsored events is prohibited.

- Press, poster and shopfront advertisements for sponsored events:

    - must comply as far as practicable with the Cigarette Code (see summary of advertising agreement, "Content of cigarette advertisements");

    - must seek primarily to direct attention to the event and venue;

    - must not depict a cigarette or a cigarette/hand-rolling tobacco pack, nor echo any elements in the design of a cigarette/hand-rolling tobacco pack/advertisement other than the house or brand name;

    - must not depict any participants in a sport, nor anybody smoking.

- Advertisements or promotional signs for sponsored events may not be displayed within 200 metres of the front entrance of schools, except where an event is taking place at a venue within that area. In the latter case, advertisements or promotional signs may be displayed during the course of the event or for up to six weeks beforehand.

Televised sporting events

- Television coverage of sponsored events is subject to Codes of Practice laid down by the BBC and ITC.

- In addition, static promotional signs at sporting events should not be located within camera sightlines for prolonged, uninterrupted periods. Signs which are likely to come within television coverage should carry only the official title of the event and a health warning.

- There are limits on the maximum number and size of signs allowed to appear in television coverage for each type of event.

- Brand names or symbols may not be displayed on participants and officials, nor their vehicles and equipment, if they are likely to come within the television coverage of an activity in the UK.

- The design of the set for small arena sports should not resemble the sponsor's product, except that promotional signs may be printed in the style and colours normally associated with the sponsor's house or brand name.

Monitoring and compliance

The Committee for Monitoring Agreements on Tobacco Advertising and Sponsorship (COMATAS) may commission independent studies to monitor compliance with the voluntary agreement.

In addition, COMATAS will investigate and respond to complaints about possible breaches of the agreement. The COMATAS address is:

The Secretariat
COMATAS
PO Box 3982
London SE1 8YJ

Copies of the agreement can be obtained from the COMATAS secretariat.

Printed in the United Kingdom for HMSO
Dd0301179 C4 7/95 3396 17434